>> CODE POWER: A TEEN PROGRAMMER'S GUIDE™

GETTING TO KNOW
Lego Mindstorms

THERESE SHEA

rosen publishing's
rosen central

NEW YORK

Published in 2015 by The Rosen Publishing Group, Inc.
29 East 21st Street, New York, NY 10010

Copyright © 2015 by The Rosen Publishing Group, Inc.

First Edition

Library of Congress Cataloging-in-Publication Data

Shea, Therese, author.
Getting to know Lego Mindstorms/Therese Shea.—First edition.
    pages cm.—(Code power: a teen programmer's guide)
Audience: Grades 5 to 8.
Includes bibliographical references and index.
ISBN 978-1-4777-7701-5 (library bound—ISBN 978-1-4777-7703-9 (pbk.)—
ISBN 978-1-4777-7704-6 (6-pack)
1. LEGO Mindstorms toys—Juvenile literature. 2. Robotics—Juvenile literature.
3. Robots—Design and construction—Juvenile literature. 4. Robots—
Programming—Juvenile literature. I. Title.
TJ211.2.S536 2015
629.8'92—dc23
                                                                2013044053

Manufactured in the United States of America

{CONTENTS

{ INTRODUCTION

J ust as spoken and written languages help people communicate with one another, programming languages exist for people to communicate with computers. As with any language, each programming language has a unique vocabulary and set of rules. Without following these conventions, the computer will either not function as the programmer wants it to or will not operate at all—like how a person might not respond if spoken to in a language he or she does not understand. You can find samples of programming code at sites such as www.happycodings.com.

Learning programming languages was once something students tackled only in college or in an accelerated high school course. However just as most computers now have a visual interface that allows people to supply commands with a click or even a touch rather than writing complicated code, it is possible to construct code in a visual way, too.

Joy of Building
Pride of Creation

>> While Lego toys and robotics kits are found in the toy sections of stores, they have fans of all ages. The EV3 Mindstorms kit, seen here, was long awaited by Lego enthusiasts.

The Lego company, the creator of the familiar brick-stacking toys, found a way to marry its construction products with technology in an accessible robotics kit. The Lego kits, called Mindstorms, contain both hardware and software. The hardware includes Lego building blocks, gears, wheels, and other pieces that interlock and connect without the use of glue and tools that other robot kits might require. Additional essential hardware includes sensors, motors, and a microprocessor that serves as the brain of the robot. The kits guide budding engineers in the making of various robots, laying the foundation for unique and more challenging projects.

Each kit also includes the Mindstorms software, which presents an easy-to-use programming technique in a visual environment. The Lego Mindstorms programming language is contained in icons called blocks. Programmers choose blocks and select configurations within them to build programs that will command their robots. Though tutorials start users with the basics, there are no bounds to the different programs that can be built. Commands can be as simple or as complicated as users choose. As users gain skill, they can experiment with more complex programs.

The Mindstorms system has already undergone several changes since its introduction in 1998, and each one is an improvement on the last, reflecting and addressing users' needs and concerns. The Mindstorms kit's designers have stuck to some guiding principles that have sealed its success. First, it is meant for multiple uses. There are an infinite number of possibilities in both hardware and software. Many other robotics kits permit only one model. Second, after the robot is built, a simple program can be downloaded to it in mere minutes.

Since Mindstorms users own similar sets, they can communicate easily, and many have formed communities online and offline that share valuable experiences and innovative ideas. Mindstorms has interested many people of all ages and backgrounds who might otherwise have felt intimidated by the technology in both the worlds of programming and robotics. The journey from the Lego brick to the Lego robot is a big step in the world of educational toys.

CHAPTER 1

THE TOY OF THE CENTURY

The incredibly popular Lego brand was founded in the 1930s by Danish carpenter Ole Kirk Kristiansen. In 1932, Kristiansen and his young son opened a workshop. Among other homemade objects, Kristiansen constructed wooden toys. In

>> A photograph of Lego founder Ole Kirk Kristiansen and his wife hangs in a Lego meeting room. Kristiansen's company has grown into one of the most popular and successful toy manufacturers in the world.

1934, he named his growing business "Lego" from the Danish words *leg* and *godt*, meaning "play well." (In Danish, Lego is pronounced LEE-go.)

In 1947, the Kristiansens were introduced to children's interlocking building bricks, which were being made in England. They decided to make a similar product. The Lego "automatic binding bricks" were hollow with pegs on top. The company began using plastic to make some of its toys and discontinued its wood products after a warehouse fire. By the late 1950s, Godfred Kristiansen, Ole's son, had perfected the Lego brick design for better stability. That classic design has not changed since 1958.

The company today is owned by Kjeld Kirk Kristiansen, the grandchild of the founder. According to Lego's official Web site, the company is the world's fourth-largest toy manufacturer and has held the title of "Toy of the Century" twice. How does Lego maintain its popularity? Lego brick sets provide instructions on how to build a specific structure, but, if the builder wants to veer off the path and construct something from his or her own imagination, the possibilities are endless. Interestingly, this same philosophy governs the Lego Mindstorms products of today.

NOT JUST A TOY

Mindstorms was born of a collaboration between the Lego company and the Massachusetts Institute of Technology (MIT), one of the most prestigious universities in the world. In 1985, Lego began sponsoring MIT's Media Lab, which was founded to research the creative use of digital technologies. Media Lab professor Mitchel Resnick was interested specifically in integrating toys and computers into a child's learning environment. In an early product used in schools, called Lego TC Logo, students could program their Lego brick creations to move using a computer, software, motors, and a connection cable.

>> MIT Media Lab professor Mitchel Resnick is shown here with an early Lego robotics product called MyBot. The MyBot contained a computer as well as light and motion sensors.

By 1998, the Media Lab had developed the first version of the "programmable brick," a kind of small battery-operated computer. Once a program was downloaded to the brick from a regular computer, the brick could control the robot. The software

for these programmable bricks used a text-based programming language called Logo, specially designed for learners.

The first commercial Mindstorms construction kits were sold in 1998. Based on MIT's technology, a tiny computer was included in the programming brick, now called the Intelligent Brick. People could build their own Lego robots and program them to interact with their surroundings using sensors and motors. The programming software shifted from using text to icons that required manipulation. This programming environment was called Legosheets. Today's Mindstorms kits include graphical programming environments as well, but text-based programming is possible, too. Though the Mindstorms Intelligent Brick and software have changed, the aim has remained the same: to provide an accessible entry into the world of robotics. And once the Mindstorms user enters that world, the possibilities are endless.

Mindstorms users are diverse. Although recommended for ages ten and up, there are younger users as well as those who are much older. Hobbyists use Mindstorms for fun, while

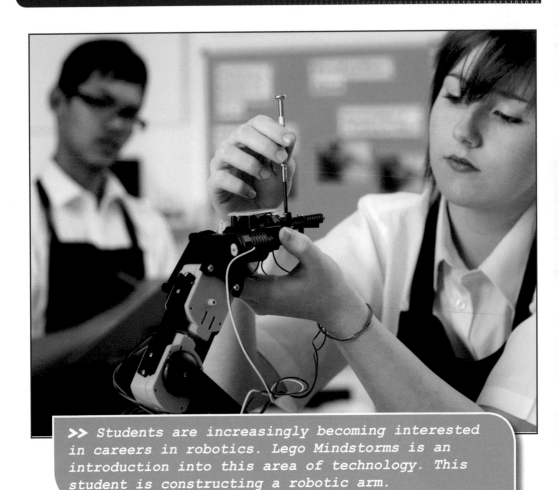

>> Students are increasingly becoming interested in careers in robotics. Lego Mindstorms is an introduction into this area of technology. This student is constructing a robotic arm.

some engineers use it to help them in their work. Some people enter competitions to show off their Mindstorms design and programming skills. Though many people buy retail sets for home use, Mindstorms Education kits, specially meant for classroom instruction, are now a part of many schools. Teachers have found that robotics is an engaging way to introduce and explore the branches of STEM (science, technology, engineering, and math) education.

>> TECHNICS AND WEDO

In 1977, Lego Technics sets were introduced as "Lego Technical Sets." Rather than just including traditional bricks, this series allowed builders to make more advanced creations with movable parts, including motors and gears. Technic pieces are used in other Lego products, including Mindstorms kits. Many Technic pieces are "studless," meaning they do not have the pegs of the traditional Lego bricks.

In 2008, Lego WeDo was introduced to answer the demand for a robot-building kit designed for younger kids. WeDo is a valuable beginning platform for young robot-builders, before they graduate to Mindstorms. Designed for ages seven to twelve, WeDo comes with software that users can easily manipulate to bring their simple models to life.

WHAT'S IN A NAME?

MIT's Media Lab credits professor Seymour Papert with planting the first seeds of Lego Mindstorms. Papert was a proponent of using computers as a vehicle for teaching children as early as the 1960s, years before affordable personal computers were on the market. Papert, in turn, was influenced by Jean Piaget, a Swiss psychologist who studied the learning processes of young children. Piaget and Papert backed the constructivist theory of learning, the idea that knowledge is created by learners through interaction with other people and the world around them.

As a professor at MIT, Papert studied how technology could be integrated into the classroom. He is the author of the book

>> Seymour Papert is a mathematician, computer scientist, and educator. He challenged traditional classrooms to weave technology into the curriculum.

Mindstorms: Children, Computers and Powerful Ideas, from which the Mindstorms name originated. A "mindstorm" refers to the energetic "storm" of activity that learners experience in a creative, self-directed, and technology-filled environment.

Papert believes the ways most teachers present math and science are too far removed from a child's experience. He is quoted on the Lego Education Web site as saying, "Children learn best when they are actively engaged in constructing something that has a personal meaning to them—be it a poem, a robot, a sandcastle, or a computer program." In Papert's research lab, he introduced young children to the Logo programming language and robotic turtles. The children "played" with these tools, using the turtles to draw pictures and solve mathematical problems in the process. Papert is still a member of the Lego advisory board.

GET STARTED

The Lego Mindstorms user guide reads: "Build. Program. Go!" Users construct a robot with the capability of interacting with the environment, write a program providing instructions to their creation, download and run the program, and then watch what happens. There is a bit more to each stage, but these are the basics of the Mindstorms kits.

The fun and challenge of the kit is the unlimited variation involved. Design is not limited to just the creations that Lego offers, and programming is not bound to the instructions in the software. However, it is recommended that beginners follow the instructions in the user guide to get a basic understanding of how the hardware and software operate before veering off in a new direction in either design or programming.

BODY BUILDERS

Since 1998, there have been three Mindstorms systems on the market: RCX, NXT, and EV3. For each, several versions have been released, including retail versions and education sets for use in classrooms. However, only the NXT and EV3 are currently supported by Lego.

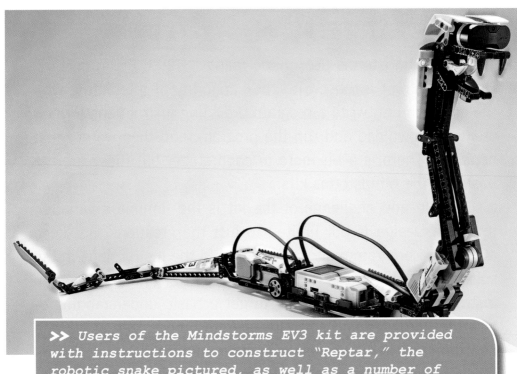

>> Users of the Mindstorms EV3 kit are provided with instructions to construct "Reptar," the robotic snake pictured, as well as a number of other robotic creations.

The EV3, the latest incarnation, was released in 2013. The "EV" stands for "evolution" and the "3" refers to its status as the third generation of Mindstorms. The EV3 Intelligent Brick is compatible with all Lego programmable bricks, motors, and sensors, and EV3 software can be used to program NXT bricks. This means that users of both NXT and EV3 can keep programs in the same EV3 application and not have to use separate applications to program different robots. However, the EV3 brick cannot be programmed with the NXT software. And, though the NXT sensors and motors will work with the EV3 brick, EV3 sensors and motors will not work with the NXT brick.

THE BRAIN IS IN THE BRICK

Every Mindstorms kit contains a programmable brick that functions as the brain of the robot. The EV3 Intelligent Brick uses an ARM 9-based processor, the most powerful microprocessor to date, that runs a Linux operating system. It is even more like an actual computer than its predecessors. A micro SD (secure digital) card slot adds a choice of storage to its already expanded memory (16 megabytes of flash memory and 64 megabytes of RAM).

The EV3 Intelligent Brick also has an LCD display with a speaker and more buttons for on-brick programming than the NXT. It can be controlled via Bluetooth using both iOS- and Android-operated smartphones. (The NXT was compatible only with Android.) The EV3 brick uses six AA batteries or a lithium rechargeable battery.

GET MOVIN'

If the Intelligent Brick is the brains of the Mindstorms robot, then the motors are the muscles. Both NXT and EV3 have ports labeled alphabetically at the top of the brick into which motors can be plugged. The EV3 contains four motor ports compared to the NXT's three. Both kits come with three motors; two are large and powerful and one is smaller and less powerful. One of the EV3's motors is designed to rotate attachments, like arms or propellers. The Intelligent Brick makes sure the motors work together, somewhat like the human brain makes sure the body's muscles do.

SENSING THE SURROUNDINGS

One reason robots are so cool is that, like people, they react to their environments. The sensors function as the senses of the robot. The NXT and EV3 Intelligent Bricks have four input ports on the bottom for attaching sensors, labeled one through four.

Sensors include a touch sensor, which the robot uses to make contact with its environment, and a color/light sensor that distinguishes colors and amounts of light. The EV3 infrared sensor detects proximity of objects and reads signals sent from an infrared beacon. The sensor, beacon, and a remote control allow users to manipulate the robot without having to create a program.

Some Mindstorms sets also have an ultrasonic sensor that uses sound waves to measure distance, up to 8 feet (2.4 meters) in the EV3. There are even companies that make unofficial sensors for Mindstorms systems, for example, sensors that measure air temperature and altitude.

>> *Sensors are located on this NXT robot's "head" and "hands." The Intelligent Brick is its torso. Motors are located at strategic positions to allow the robot to move efficiently.*

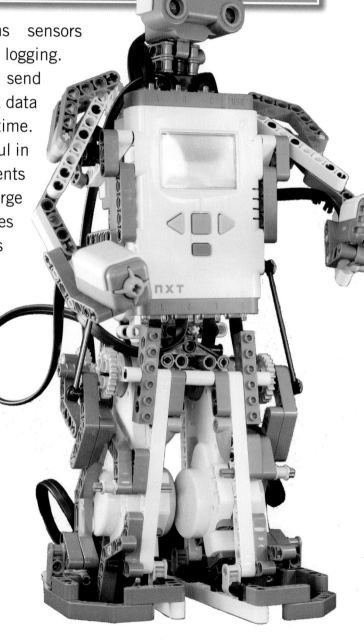

The Mindstorms sensors also aid in data logging. That means they send the Intelligent Brick data collected for a later time. This would be helpful in scientific experiments dealing with a very large amount of figures or measurements that are too difficult for humans to record without the aid of tools—for example, the temperature of an environment or the speed of an object. After the data is uploaded to a computer, the data file can be used to make graphs and charts.

>> INTERVIEW WITH A MINDSTORMS EDUCATOR

Name: Jonathan Dietz
School: Weston Middle School, Weston, Massachusetts
Position: Technology/Engineering Teacher, Grades 7 and 8
Classes in which you use Lego Mindstorms: Lego Robotics (Grade 7); Advanced Lego Robotics (Grade 8)

Describe how Lego Mindstorms has affected your teaching methods.

The Lego robotics system enables us to teach computer programming, mechanical design, and issues in current technology in a project-based format that is fun and engaging. It lends itself to differentiated instruction and varying levels of student ability. Struggling students may build designs from kits and make only modest changes to sample programs, while advanced students may complete complex, original designs with highly sophisticated programming. Also, the parts are rugged and fully reusable, keeping ongoing operating costs to a minimum.

Are there other robotics kits you use?

While not a kit system, in the past year we have experimented with building Arduino-based robots and hope to continue this work. However, these have proven somewhat challenging for students without prior programming experience, at least at the middle school level.

What are your impressions of the Mindstorms programming software? Do you use other programming software/environments?

Positives: The Mindstorms NXT-G programming environment is readily learned by most students, both at the introductory level (grade 7) and advanced level (grade 8). The ability to comment on screen is helpful.

Negatives: The built-in instructional material in NXT-G has not been helpful. The Education version does not include the sound recording capability included in the retail version (a feature often requested by students). The memory in the NXT is limited, causing out-of-memory errors, particularly when using the data collection features.

Other software: We have not used other software (such as LabVIEW) with the Mindstorms system as they seemed too complex for most students at the middle school level and did not add significant functionality. For students interested in advanced programming, we have been using the Arduino environment as it is closely related to mainstream programming languages such as C++ and Python.

Do you have any further comments about the impact of Lego Mindstorms, in particular the programming?

The Mindstorms system has opened the minds of many students to both the possibilities of careers in technology and computer science, and, at the very least, has given students some understanding of how devices in their computer-filled worlds are designed and programmed as well as the engineering design process.

THE BONES OF THE BOT

Muscles need to be attached to bones to move the body, and so the Mindstorms motors are attached to Lego pieces. While there are 206 bones in the human body, both the EV3 and the NXT sets come with close to 600 Lego Technic pieces, including beams, plates, gears, hinges, tubing, wheel hubs, tires, and wire bricks.

Each Mindstorms kit contains instructions for more than one robot. The EV3 has directions for five different robots, including a snake, a scorpion, and a humanoid, and seventeen others are available online. The EV3 offers both paper and downloadable 3D instructions, neither of which had been available to NXT owners.

>> Duncan Titmarsh is a professional Lego builder. With permission and materials coming from the Lego company, people pay Titmarsh to design and build artwork and sculptures, such as a life-size tiger and even a house.

Mindstorms instructions are mostly illustrations using labeled pieces and visual directives about how they fit together. Because there are so many small and similar looking pieces, mistakes can happen in the building process. Errors are why Lego experts recommend tackling each project by building subassemblies. This means building several smaller parts of the robot first and then assembling them into the larger structure. Subassemblies can help reduce frustration. The builder may need to take apart only one subassembly rather than the whole structure to amend an incorrect placement. Building this way also makes the robot easy to take apart, transport, and reattach in other locations, for example, robotics classes, clubs, and competitions.

Mindstorms users should know that improving mechanical design is a normal part of the process, especially if they're building something unique, just as it is for real-life engineers. Builders need to account for the shape and placement of the motors and sensors. Other factors to consider include the height and mass of the robot. A tall robot can be unstable. A heavy robot may not perform well, either. The positioning of the Intelligent Brick, the heaviest component, is important, for example. Too much weight over a caster will cause mobility problems. Always be prepared for trial and error, but a little planning helps, too.

BOSSING THE BOT

So, the robot has a brain, muscles, bones, and senses. Now it just needs instructions. This is where the programming comes in. The first thing Mindstorms users need to know is that they do not even have to turn on their computers to run their robot. They can tell it what to do using the Intelligent Brick. It is possible to program the Lego robot using the buttons on the brick; the programmer can just scroll through the available options. The EV3 offers more on-brick programming than in the past. However, these programs will still be fairly simple so most users will want to dive into the software eventually.

Each generation of Mindstorms software has employed a visual programming environment. The developers of the original Legosheet software had found that users lost interest in programming when code became too confusing, so the developers decided to use graphical representations of code instead. The RCX used the specially made RCX graphical code as well as ROBOLAB, a visual programming language built in LabVIEW that was developed by Tufts University's Center for Engineering Education and Outreach for educational Lego robotics.

ROBOLAB provided inspiration for the official NXT icon-based programming environment, called NXT-G. The "G" stands for "graphical." Optionally, Lego also offers LabVIEW for Lego Mindstorms, software created by the National Instruments company, which develops similar intuitive software for engineers and scientists. As of the time of this writing, the EV3 only comes bundled with the EV3 software platform. However, LabVIEW plans to develop a product for the EV3 as well.

BE THE SOFTWARE ENGINEER

After the Mindstorms software is installed on a computer, users click on the program icon to open the application and begin to write programs. The first step before actually writing a program is to figure out what the robot should do. Next, either draw the moves and responses of the robot in a diagram or write them down in ordinary language. Engineers would call this creating an algorithm. Finally, follow this plan to convert the instructions into a program. After the

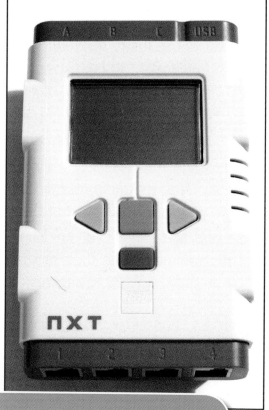

>> While this NXT Intelligent Brick has four buttons, the EV3 has six, providing even more programming options.

program is done, all the programmer has to do is save it, download it to the Intelligent Brick, and run it. Occasionally, systems can crash, so users should always name each program so they can easily find it later and save it often so they do not lose too much of their work.

Programs created using the software can be downloaded to the robot via the Intelligent Brick's USB port. Connectivity options include a USB cable and, in the case of the EV3, a Wi-Fi dongle placed in the port. (It should be noted that Wi-Fi takes more time and battery power than the USB cable.) Data collected from the robot can be uploaded to the computer in the same way. In the EV3, a Bluetooth wireless connection allows a user to use his or her handheld device, such as an iPhone, iPad, or iPod Touch, to control the robot.

Both Mindstorms NXT-G and EV3 programming software employ a "drag and drop" user interface. This means programmers manipulate blocks that represent code on their screen with their mouse, dragging the blocks and placing them on the application's work area. The work area always contains a start point, and the blocks are placed to the right of this, in a linear direction. Blocks lock in place, sort of like Lego bricks. Each block contains commands, and programmers write their program as a sequence of commands. A complete program can be one block or many.

PICKING FROM THE PALETTE

Just as an artist chooses paints from a palette, the Mindstorms programmer chooses command blocks from a palette—a programming palette. The Mindstorms programming language uses dozens of blocks, and all can be found in the Complete Palette. However, the most commonly used blocks are located in the Common Palette, which is placed to the left of the work area in NXT software and on the bottom in EV3. These blocks are Move, Record/Play, Sound, Wait, Display, Loop, and Switch. Using just these programming blocks can allow users to develop programs that command robots to change position, play sounds, display text and graphics on the Intelligent Brick's LCD, collect data from sensors, and apply input to control robot behavior.

The programmer determines specific functions within each block, some of which are set by default. In the NXT software, these functions are viewed and altered in the Configuration Panel for each block. In the EV3 software, each block has icons on it representing functions, so users can see all the information in their program at once, without having to click on each block.

MOVE BLOCK

In the Move block, the programmer controls the movements of the robot through its motors. Specifications on this block allow the user to program which motors are used (motor ports are labeled for this reason), the direction of the robot, the amount of power (spin speed of the motor), and the duration of the move- ment. He or she also chooses whether the robot's movements will be calculated by seconds, degrees, or rotations of the wheels.

For example, a programmer can drag and drop a Move block in the work area and set the robot to roll forward a duration of eighty rotations at a power setting of 50. If the power setting was moved up to 100, the robot would move a lot faster for

>> *This forklift was created with the Mindstorms NXT kit. Not only do its motors move the machine, they also lift and lower the fork.*

those eighty rotations but also use more battery power. Robots can move in circles and be set to brake quickly or coast to a stop via the Move block, too.

RECORD/PLAY BLOCK

The Record/Play block is used to record motor movement to a file and play it back. Users can record a single motor port or all ports, as well as determine how long the recording should be. The recording time should be as precise as possible since the Intelligent Brick has limited memory.

For example, a programmer could drop this block to the work area and set it to record ten seconds. Then, the programmer would download the program to the brick and run it. Now, he or she has ten seconds to move the robot manually. The robot's motor movements during that time are recorded and stored.

To play it back, the programmer opens a new program, drops the Record/Play block on the work area, chooses "play" on the block this time, and then selects the stored file. Finally, the programmer downloads this new program and runs it. The robot's motors will move as the programmer had moved it before.

SOUND BLOCK

The Sound block is used to play a sound file or musical tone out of the Intelligent Brick's speaker. The programmer can select whether to make the robot repeat a prerecorded sound file, such as a voice saying "good-bye" or a musical note of the user's choice. Musical tones can be selected using a graphical keyboard. The programmer also determines how long the note will play. Other settings to choose on the Sound block include volume, repeat, and wait, which means that further programming on the chain of commands will not commence until the completion of the sound.

This option could be handy for several reasons. Imagine two programmers wanted to race their robots. They might agree to begin their program with a horn sound for three seconds and follow that with the Move block of their specifications.

WAIT BLOCK

Many Mindstorms blocks have a time function, but sometimes a programmer wants a robot to keep moving or doing something until a condition is met. The Wait block is used to delay blocks in the programming sequence for a period of time or prevent execution of programming until data input from a sensor fulfills a predetermined condition. Depending on which way the block is used, it may be called the Time Wait block or the Sensor Wait block.

For example, a programmer could add a Wait block to the program after a Move block and configure the Wait block so that the robot will stop moving after sixty seconds. Or, the programmer could set the block to be a Sensor Wait and keep motors running until a color sensor detects a red light.

DISPLAY BLOCK

The Display block is used to display a graphic or text

>> Creating a simple program on the Intelligent Brick using the buttons and display is a great way to get to know what a Lego robot can do. Most users will then want to tackle something more complicated.

on the Intelligent Brick's LCD. Choices for this block include different pictures and shapes to show, including unique drawings, messages that can be typed into a text box, the positioning of objects and words on the display, and whether the display should be cleared of other text and images. Alternatively, the Display block can be used to reset the display so that it shows the standard Intelligent Brick menu.

For example, if a programmer has a robot in a competition, he or she might want to put the robot's name on the Intelligent Brick's screen or display a message for the other competitors,

>> DATA WIRES

Data wires are a way for blocks to share information. A wire connects certain blocks, taking output data from one and using it as input data for another. Data wires are different colors depending on the data type, such as number, text, and logic (for instance, true/false commands). They can split and share information with two blocks. They can carry information from the last block of the program to the first.

Data wires can get confusing. They do not have to be a part of the program, but they are available because they can help programmers create interesting, complicated code. Users should remember that just as the process of building a unique Mindstorms robot may call for some redesigning, the process of programming a robot may include some rewriting and reprogramming.

For more information on blocks, data wires, and more, be sure to read the many excellent Mindstorms programming guides both online and at the library.

such as "Victory is mine!" The programmer can use the Wait block to determine how long that message will remain on the screen.

LOOP BLOCK

The Loop block repeats the execution of one or more programming blocks continuously until a predefined condition is met. This block saves Mindstorms programmers a lot of time. For example, if the programmer wants the robot to dance, a loop will help. Most dances are a set number of movements performed again and again. A programmer's robot dance might have three moves: A Move block makes the robot move left two wheel

>> Both design and programming are crucial skills in competitions such as the World Robot Olympiad. Entrants' robotics programs can be quite advanced.

rotations. Another Move block makes it move backward three wheel rotations. Yet another makes it move in a complete circle. The Loop block can make these moves happen over and over without the programmer repeating the pattern in the work area.

First, the three Move blocks must be dragged into the Loop (which will expand) and then arranged in the correct order. Next, the programmer selects how long the actions should loop: forever (until the brick's batteries lose power); until a condition is met with a sensor's data; a period of time; a number of times; or until a logic requirement is fulfilled (whether certain data is true or false).

SWITCH BLOCK

The Switch block of programming is called a conditional block. It essentially "tests" for one or more conditions, based on input data. One could also say the Switch helps a robot make a decision during a program. If one condition is true, then the robot will perform one action. And if the condition is false, then the robot will execute another block of programming. In the Switch, the top path is what happens if the set condition is true and the bottom if it is false. The programmer creates two separate sequences.

For example, a programmer can link the Switch to a color sensor and set the condition as the detection of the color yellow. If the sensor "sees" yellow, the robot will turn right. If it does not, it will go straight. Programmers can add more options as well. The Switch block is an introduction into the world of variable programming, which advanced programmers deal with all the time.

BLOCKS UPON BLOCKS

There are even more blocks than the seven in this section. Users do not need to memorize them, as they might have to know other kinds of text-based code. Both NXT and EV3 software offer a step-by-step guide to familiarize users with the blocks and with using them to write programs. And, if users are still unsure what a block or an icon does, they can place their cursor over it. Words will pop up on the screen outlining its functions. Each block has symbols on it that help remind users what it is and what it does.

Programmers can download new blocks from Web sites and even make their own. This enables them to reuse a sequence of programming as a single block without having to rewrite the sequence each time. Lego encourages this and even includes a Custom Palette within the Complete Palette folder, so programmers have a place to store their blocks.

CHAPTER 4

MEETING OF THE MINDSTORMERS

Once Mindstorms users know the basics of programming, they can do a lot. We already know programs can move robots, command them to make noise, record, and more, but there are so many more possibilities. Mindstorms enthusiasts can make and program a robot or machine that follows a line, works like a forklift, plays baseball, functions as a radar, or even moves like a dolphin. The instructions to do all of these things can be found online. When Mindstorms users are looking for a new project or are stuck on a difficult piece of code, they are lucky that they can tap into the enthusiasm and creativity of a large and helpful community.

MINGLING IN THE MINDSTORMS COMMUNITY

Lego hosts an official community forum on its Web site, but many other online communities exist as well, such as MINDboards. Both are welcoming sites where people can share information, videos, and photographs; offer helpful building and programming hints; and even brag a bit about their accomplishments.

>> A team cheers on their creations in a Lego building challenge in San Francisco, Calif. One of these baseball-playing robots was a pitcher and another a batter.

Other Web sites host podcasts that have more information about Mindstorms projects. There are also Mindstorms clubs and workshops at schools, libraries, churches, and community centers. Some people start their own groups when there are none to be found in their neighborhoods.

>> THE ROBOTICS INSTITUTE

People interested in robots can pursue a career in the field at Carnegie Mellon University's Robotics Institute, established in 1979. It was the first robotics department in any American university. The world's first robotics Ph.D. program was founded there in 1988. Since then, the Robotics Institute has produced many research successes in intelligent manufacturing, self-directed vehicles, space-related robots, medical robotics, and anthropomorphic robots. It also offers programs, workshops, and summer classes for young robotics enthusiasts. Graduates from the Ph.D. program teach at universities or work in the industry, including designing and controlling NASA Mars rovers.

The Robotics Institute currently has more than five hundred faculty, staff, and students. The institute's Robotics Academy is an educational arm of Carnegie Mellon University and is committed to motivating students to pursue careers in the fields of science and technology.

>> NASA's rover Curiosity used navigation software to drive itself on the surface of Mars. This software was developed at Carnegie Mellon University's Robotics Institute.

MASTERING MINDSTORMS AT SCHOOL

In the classroom, despite numerous changes to the kits over the years, the Mindstorms product has remained true to the theory of education that says constructing projects is how people learn best. Lego designs Mindstorms programs for classrooms, more than thirty hours of instruction and activities, but the versatility of the kits far exceeds this time limit. Mindstorms Education kits have given teachers the tools to interest students with everything from simple machines, such as pulleys, to structural engineering concepts such as tension, bracing, and loading limitations—and, of course, computer programming.

In an interview with *Smithsonian* magazine, one college student described Mindstorms as a "sneaky" way to educate, meaning the kit is more about fun to the user than design, construction, and programming. Perhaps that is why, as of the time of this writing, about one-half of all middle schools and about one-quarter of all elementary and high schools in the continental United States use Mindstorms in their classrooms.

BATTLING 'BOTS

Many young Mindstorms enthusiasts enter contests and tournaments in which they build and program a robot to tackle a specified task. In the United States, many competitions are run by FIRST® (For Inspiration and Recognition of Science and Technology), which is a nonprofit organization founded by Dean Kamen, the creator of the Segway two-wheeled electric vehicle.

>> A team showcases their Lego wind turbine. Their project reflects their understanding of wind energy as well as related engineering concepts.

According to a Brandeis University study cited in *Smithsonian* magazine, young people who take part in robotics competitions are two times more likely to pursue a science and technology career and almost four times as likely to study engineering. According to Kamen, "The robot is just a vehicle. But by building robots, you can build self-confidence and a serious understanding of what life is like for people who work on and solve complex problems." Every spring, FIRST holds championships in four divisions. In the 2013 challenge, nearly 650 teams participated and more than $16 million in scholarships was awarded.

JUNIOR FIRST LEGO LEAGUE

Junior FIRST Lego League (Jr.FLL) is for children ages six to nine working in teams of two to six with an adult coach. The yearly challenge is related to a real world problem and requires research and critical thinking to complete. Each competition has two parts: the Lego model, a simple machine using at least one motorized piece, and the "Show Me" poster that reflects what the team studied and how they worked together to develop their model.

For example, a recent Jr.FLL challenge was called "Disaster Blaster." Participants were required to learn about natural disasters and build a model reflecting their studies. Teams may use Lego WeDo kits.

FIRST LEGO LEAGUE

First Lego League (FLL) is for ages nine to sixteen. Each FLL challenge includes a robot game and a project. Teams of up to ten participants design, construct, and program a robot using Mindstorms to solve a set of missions in the game, which is connected to the annual theme. Teams also choose and solve a problem facing the world in a project portion of the challenge. The goal of each competition is to help teammates envision themselves improving the lives of others through addressing actual problems.

For example, in response to the theme "Senior Solutions," a Maryland middle school team made a robotic arm called the

"Gramma-Jamma." This invention helps the elderly grab small objects that are out of reach.

FIRST TECH CHALLENGE

The FIRST Tech Challenge (FTC) is for students in grades seven through twelve. Teams—including coaches, mentors, and volunteers—create robots to compete against other teams in a sports-related game. Teams use a kit called TETRIX in addition to Lego Mindstorms systems. Since teams are competing against each other, not only are design and programming important, but strategy is as well. The game changes each year

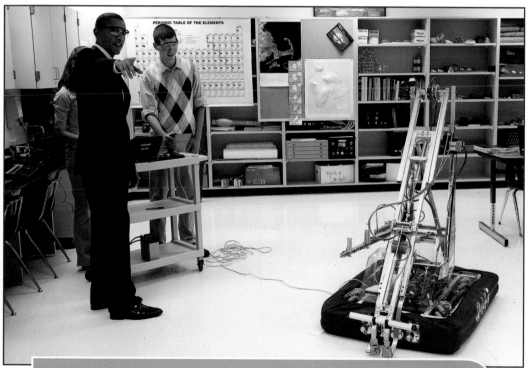

>> Students from team Carpe Robotum show President Barack Obama their FIRST robot. It can pick up and hang different-sized tubes in a specific order and at specified heights.

so teams have to build robots that can meet new challenges. Qualifying and championship tournaments lead to the World Championship.

One recent game was called "Ring It Up!" Robots had to place rings of a certain weight on a corner goal. This required that a robot be able to pick up the rings, weigh them, and move to the goal.

OTHER EVENTS

In the FIRST Robotics Competition (FRC), teams of twenty-five students or more raise funds, design a team brand, sharpen teamwork skills, and design, build, and program robots to perform tasks against a field of competitors. Volunteer professional engineers mentor each team. Robots are built in six weeks from a common kit of parts and typically weigh up to 150 pounds (68 kilograms). While Mindstorms is not a part of the FRC kit, the previous Mindstorms-related competitions help competitors to branch out into using other robotics tools and software.

Lego also sponsors the World Robot Olympiad (WRO) in which schools are invited to enter a team of three students, up to the age of nineteen, to compete in different categories of competition. One contest requires a team to build a robot to solve a challenge set on a table. Another calls for teams to create, design, and build a robot model that looks and behaves like a human athlete playing soccer.

CHAPTER 5

EVOLVING WITH THE EV3

As successful as the Mindstorms kits have been, they have gotten some criticism from users. Many of the changes from the NXT to the EV3 software were the result of Lego responding to user opinions. In fact, Lego asked a dozen nonemployees to help develop the new product, meaning the company wanted the input of the actual people who were using Mindstorms so a better system could be created. This is typical of the Lego development model.

In 2005, Lego searched online for adult users willing to be part of a user panel to test the NXT kit. The chosen panel and Lego engineers spent nearly a year swapping information and advice. (In return for their contributions, the user panel got paid in Lego pieces!)

MODIFICATIONS AND IMPROVEMENTS

One criticism that users have is that they cannot get their robots built and running as quickly as Lego claims they should be able to. Rather than thirty minutes, some need several hours to fully construct and program their first robot, even with directions.

>> Participants examine the creations brought to the "Robo Lunch Party" in San Francisco. Companies such as Facebook, Flickr, and Pandora showed off robots.

Some EV3 changes are supposed to help users build their robots even faster. The EV3 motors are shaped to facilitate design. The EV3 also contains two types of smaller wheels in addition to the larger in the NXT kit.

The EV3 color sensor is another notable change. The sensor can detect seven colors as opposed to the NXT sensor's six. In addition, according to Lego, the EV3 sensors can return new values 1,000 times per second, whereas the NXT sensors return values at 333 times per second.

The EV3 Intelligent Brick's expanded memory should improve users' experiences, too. In previous versions, after a handful of programs were downloaded to the brick, users would have to delete some to make space for new ones. That should not happen as often with the EV3.

The EV3 software is meant to be even more user friendly, too. The new environment is thought to help programmers manage complicated data wires better than the NXT. And including the configurations on each block itself should help users find and fix mistakes much quicker.

TEXT OR GRAPHICAL PROGRAMMING?

Another point of controversy is the Mindstorms graphical programming environment itself: Should it be graphical? Some critics say that the graphics can be tedious for users trying to create advanced programs. Others say that it is more valuable to teach users text-based programming languages.

In a Wired.com article, Chris Anderson wrote that young people should learn traditional coding languages rather than use graphical representations like Mindstorms' blocks. He admitted that the Mindstorms software is great for learning the basics of programming, but more ambitious users will have difficulty tackling a more complicated program using the provided software. Anderson wrote that a text-based programming language would offer more options and real-world applications than a graphical environment.

Many long-time users agree that Mindstorms' supplied software is somewhat restrictive. For this reason, text-based programming languages have been created for use with the

Mindstorms NXT, including LeJos, Not eXactly C (NXC), NeXT Byte Codes (NBC), and RobotC.

RobotC was developed by the Carnegie Mellon Robotics Academy. It allows NXT to run programs quickly and compresses files in the Intelligent Brick. Like other NXT languages, RobotC requires that special firmware be downloaded in order to run. With the introduction of Mindstorms EV3, the developers of Mindstorms-associated languages rushed to adapt to the new system.

ASSESSING THE EV3

One of the major criticisms of the Mindstorms kits was not fixed with EV3. That was price. In fact, the EV3 is the most expensive Mindstorms kit to date at about $350. In addition, users will likely want to invest in more motors and sensors after a time, increasing the cost.

Other critics are unhappy that Wi-Fi connectivity is not built into the brick. Some say that the battery and USB ports are difficult to access in completed robots. Still others complain about the Lego pieces themselves. Several can only be told apart by the number of holes along their lengths. Reviewers have also noted that mixing the studless EV3 pieces with non-Technic Lego bricks is not easy.

However, even with these evaluations, professional critics such as *PC Magazine* agree that the product is the best available on the market to teach people about building and programming robots. This opinion is due to the kit's power, memory, flexibility, and accessibility.

>> AN INTERVIEW WITH A MINDSTORMS EDUCATOR

Name: Bill Church
Schools: Littleton High School (2000–2012)
Profile School (Grades 7–12)
Plymouth State University
Position: Teacher; director of White Mountain Science, Inc. (WMSI), a nonprofit organization to support STEAM (Science, Technology, Engineering, Arts, and Math) education in northern New Hampshire
Classes in which you use Lego Mindstorms:
Physical Science (Grade 9); Physics (Grades 11, 12); Robotics (Grades 10, 11, 12); STEAM (project-based course for grades 11, 12); Astrobiology (Plymouth State University course called Life in the Universe)

Describe how Lego Mindstorms has affected your teaching methods.

The Lego Mindstorms system allows students to iterate their ideas and not be shut down when an idea "fails." It's always possible to start over. The only cost incurred is time. Iteration and failure are an essential part of science.

While the Lego system is constrained to certain types of design, the Lego geometry still allows for a myriad of possibilities. Students can customize their projects to fit their ideas and style. This is essential because students can own their designs, which means they are investing more of themselves in the class.

(continue on page 48)

(continued from page 47)

The Lego system allows for repeatable/transparent design. With structural elements that have no "tricks" in assembly and with graphical programming elements, it is easy for students to communicate and share their ideas.

It is almost the perfect tool for learning experimental and applied science. Out of the box, you have structural elements to build your project. You have sensors for measurement and durable motors for actuation, and you have an easy-to-use and easy-to-read programming environment. Finally, you have data logging and data display built into the programming environment.

What kind of design/engineering projects do your students tackle?

A) Lab activities that allow students to explore science definitions. For example, students explore velocity and acceleration by making a robot vehicle move at different rates.

B) Inquiry labs. For example, students explore a model of an unknown landscape by only looking at light data or ultrasonic data.

C) Design labs. For example, students design and program a Lego/PVC Pipe/Tetrix robot that stands 5 feet (1.52 meters) tall and can track a human wearing a red marker.

What are your impressions of the Mindstorms programming software?

Limited icons are good. Students do not feel that they need to learn a million new things to get started. They only need to know two—a motor command and a wait for sensor value command.

Icons with controllable features are great. The new Mindstorms system [EV3] took a major step in making these visible in the programming environment. Debugging is now easier because you can see potential mistakes. You can also see where the program is as it is being executed. This gives students a better mental model of program flow.

The new system also helps with the classic "port bug" because it automatically identifies the motors and sensors.

The new software also has more math functions and a graph programming feature. I want students to see the changing values of their sensors in a science investigation or engineering project. The better they can "see" what their sensors see, the more confident they can be in their designs.

Finally, the new software has an interactive activity guide feature that is editable. Students can use it to document their projects by inserting text, images, and links. Teachers can scaffold their students' learning experiences by making interactive guides to help students move through multi-step/multi-phase projects at their own pace.

I use the Mindstorms software when I am working with upper elementary and middle school students as well as teachers that are new to robotics. For high school students and experienced teachers, I use LabVIEW. It is the next level of programming that is an industry standard development environment.

Do you plan on switching to EV3?

Yes, I plan on switching to the EV3 because of its faster processor, expanded memory, additional motor port automatic sensor ID, Wi-Fi and other USB peripheral options, and Linux core. As the EV3 has a Linux computer, developers will be able to help the EV3 "keep up with the times" by updating the operating system and software apps.

MINDSTORMS' EXPANDING IMPACT

Beyond the toy room, the classroom, and the competition arenas, Mindstorms has implications for the business world, too. Engineers use kits to create prototypes for ingenious inventions. In a recent story on NPR.org, software engineer Will Gorman of San Francisco reported using Mindstorms systems to create a Nintendo Wii–playing robot and a prototype of the Mars *Curiosity* rover built by NASA. They are used for prototypes for everything from medical robots to toilet flushers. Similarly, robotic models have been made for the United States Postal Service. Silicon Valley engineers were as eager as young Mindstorms users to get their hands on the new EV3 kits.

>> *Ngee Ann Polytechnic in Singapore uses LEGO Mindstorms to equip students with hands-on skills in simple robotics applications.*

Mindstorms is not limited to U.S. schools and businesses. Ngee Ann Polytechnic Institution's School of Engineering in Singapore used Mindstorms NXT to create a vision-guided robot to collect tennis balls. By using a camera to acquire images and a program to perform object tracking, the machine successfully performed its task. While it is not large enough to operate on an actual tennis court, the machine demonstrated that larger machines could be successfully made.

In 1963, Godfred Kristiansen presented the ten characteristics of every Lego product:

Unlimited play potential
For girls and for boys
Fun for every age
Year-round play
Healthy, quiet play
Long hours of play
Development, imagination, creativity
The more Lego, the greater the value
Extra sets available
Quality in every detail

More than fifty years later, these qualities speak not only for the iconic Lego brick but for the Lego Mindstorms systems. The engineers of tomorrow and today find Lego Mindstorms a playground for their intelligence and creativity.

ALGORITHM A step-by-step procedure for solving a problem that can be translated into a computer program.

ANTHROPOMORPHIC Having human form or characteristics.

ARDUINO A single-board microcontroller used in electronics projects. Arduino boards can be purchased preassembled or as do-it-yourself kits.

ARM A 32-bit microprocessor developed by Advanced RISC Machines, Ltd. in the 1980s.

BEACON A radio transmitter that continuously broadcasts a signal that some machines use for guidance.

BRACING Using devices to hold a structure steady or upright.

CASTER A small wheel on a mount that allows it to turn in all directions.

DONGLE A small hardware device that, when plugged into a computer, enables a program to run.

FIRMWARE A set of computer instructions stored permanently in a computer's hardware rather than as part of a program.

FLASH MEMORY A special type of electronic storage that can be easily erased and reprogrammed.

INFRARED Using or producing the part of the invisible electromagnetic spectrum between light and radio waves.

INPUT Data entered into a computer.

INTELLIGENT Programmed to be able to adjust to environmental changes and to make conclusions from processed information.

ITERATION A process of achieving a desired result by repeating a sequence of steps and getting closer to that result.

LINUX A free open-source operating system that runs on a number of hardware platforms, including PCs and Macs.

LCD Short for liquid crystal display. A type of display used in many portable computers.

MICROPROCESSOR A chip that contains a CPU (central processing unit) contained in all personal computers.

OUTPUT Information produced by a computer.

PROTOTYPE Something that has the essential features of a later type, and on which later types are modeled.

RAM Random-access memory. A RAM disk has been set up to act as a disk drive.

ROVER A small vehicle used to explore the surface of a planet.

TORQUE Force that causes rotation, twisting, or turning.

USB Universal serial bus. An external collection of wires between a computer and a device through which data is transmitted.

Association for Unmanned Vehicle Systems International
1735 North Lynn Street
Suite 950
Arlington, VA 22209-2022
(703) 524-6646
Website: http://www.auvsi.org
This global organization promotes the advancement of
    unmanned vehicles. Student membership is available.

FIRST
200 Bedford Street
Manchester, NH 03101
(800) 871-8326
Website: http://www.usfirst.org
This is the official site of the FIRST organization, the
    masterminds behind the Mindstorms robotics
    competitions.

FIRST Canada
P.O. Box 518
Pickering Main
Pickering, ON L1V2R7
Canada
(416) 283-7659
Website: http://www.firstroboticscanada.org
FIRST Canada's mission is to inspire young people to study
    science, technology, and engineering.

Institute of Electrical and Electronics Engineers
Robotics and Automation Society
501 Hoes Lane
Piscataway, NJ 08854
(732) 562 3906
Website: http://www.ieee-ras.org
The IEEE Robotics and Automation Society seeks to
    advance the theory and practice of robotics in the world.

Lego Systems, Inc.
555 Taylor Road
P.O. Box 1138
Enfield, CT 06083-1138
(800) 835-4386
Website: http://mindstorms.lego.com
Check out all the news of the Lego company, including devel-
    opments in the WeDo, Technic, and Mindstorms products.

Ottawa Robotics Enthusiasts
Algonquin College
1385 Woodroffe Avenue
Ottawa, ON K2G 1V8
Canada
Website: http://www.ottawarobotics.org
The Ottawa Robotics Enthusiasts club is a group of hobbyist
    robotics engineers that get together to show off creations
    and share information.

The Robotics Institute
5000 Forbes Avenue
Pittsburgh, PA 15213-3890
(412) 268-3818
Website: http://www.ri.cmu.edu/index.html
Carnegie Mellon's Robotics Institute is a leader in the world of
   robotics.

WEBSITES

Due to the changing nature of Internet links, Rosen Publishing
has developed an online list of websites related to the subject of
this book. This site is updated regularly. Please use this link to
access the list:

http://www.rosenlinks.com/CODE/Lego

Baichtal, John. *Basic Robot Building with Lego Mindstorms Nxt 2.0*. Indianapolis, IN: Que, 2013.

Baichtal, John. *Make: Lego and Arduino Projects*. Sebastopol, CA: O'Reilly Media, Inc., 2012.

Bascomb, Neal. *The New Cool: A Visionary Teacher, His FIRST Robotics Team, and the Ultimate Battle of Smarts*. New York, NY: Crown Publishers, 2011.

Bender, Jonathan. *Lego: A Love Story*. Hoboken, NJ: Wiley, 2010.

Benedettelli, Daniele. *The Lego Mindstorms EV3 Laboratory*. San Francisco, CA: No Starch Press, 2013.

Bishop, Robert H. *Learning with LabVIEW 8*. Upper Saddle River, NJ: Pearson Prentice Hall, 2007.

Clay, Kathryn. *Battling for Victory: The Coolest Robot Competitions*. North Mankato, MN: Capstone Press, 2014.

Forest, Christopher. *Robot Competitions*. Mankato, MN: Capstone Press, 2013.

Gura, Mark. *Getting Started with Lego Robotics: A Guide for K–12 Educators*. Eugene, OR: International Society for Technology in Education, 2011.

Herman, Sarah. *A Million Little Bricks: The Unofficial Illustrated History of the Lego Phenomenon*. New York, NY: Skyhorse Publishing, 2012.

Hughes, Cameron, et. al. *Build Your Own Teams of Robots with Lego Mindstorms NXT and Bluetooth*. New York, NY: McGraw-Hill Education, 2013.

Isogawa, Yoshihito. *Fantastic Contraptions*. San Francisco, CA: No Starch Press, 2011.

Kelly, James Floyd. *Lego Mindstorms NXT One-Kit Wonders: Ten Inventions to Spark Your Imagination*. San Francisco, CA: No Starch Press, 2009.

Rollins, Mark. *Practical Lego Technics: Bring Your Lego Creations to Life*. New York, NY: Springer Science+Business Media, 2013.

Shea, Therese. *The Robotics Club: Teaming Up to Build Robots*. New York, NY: Rosen Central, 2011.

Trobaugh, James. *Winning Design! Lego Mindstorms NXT Design Patterns for Fun and Competition*. New York, NY: Springer Science+Business Media, 2010.

Trobaugh, James. *Winning Lego Mindstorms Programming*. New York, NY: Apress, 2012.

Wilczynski, Vince. *FIRST Robots: Behind the Design*. Gloucester, MA: Rockport Publishers, 2007.

Woodford, Chris. *Cool Stuff 2.0 and How It Works*. New York, NY: DK Publishing, 2010.

Anderson, Chris. "The Best Programming Language for Lego Mindstorms, Hands Down." Wired.com, November 12, 2007. Retrieved September 1, 2013 (http://www.wired .com/geekdad/2007/11/the-best-progra).

Baichtal, John. "12 Surprising Details About Lego Mindstorms EV3." Maker Media, August 9, 2013. Retrieved August 15, 2013 (http://makezine.com/2013/08/09/ 12-surprising-details-about-Lego-mindstorms-ev3).

Bumgardner, Jim. "The Origins of Mindstorms." Wired.com, March 29, 2007. Retrieved July 21, 2013 (http://www .wired.com/geekdad/2007/03/the_origins_of_).

Carnegie Mellon Robotics Academy. "About the Academy." Carnegie Mellon University. Retrieved September 5, 2013 (http://www.education.rec.ri.cmu.edu/content/home/ sub_pages/about/index.htm).

Church, William. Interview by author. E-mail correspondence. September 4, 2013.

CNET Editors. "Building Our First Lego Mindstorms EV3 Robot, Coming September 1 with iOS/Android Support." CNET, August 1, 2013. Retrieved August 9, 2013 (http://reviews .cnet.com/robots-and-robot-kits/Lego-mindstorms-ev3/ 4505-3510_7-35825891.html).

Davis, Brian. "Beginning Datalogging with the Lego Mindstorms NXT." Team Hassenplug. Retrieved August 30, 2013 (http://www.teamhassenplug.org/NXT/DataLogging/ Beginning_Datalogging.htm).

Dietz, Jonathan. Interview by author. E-mail correspondence. September 6, 2013.

FIRST. "First Progression of Programs." USFIRST.org. Retrieved August 17, 2013 (http://www.usfirst.org/roboticsprograms).

Greenwald, Will. "Lego Mindstorms EV3 Review and Rating." PCmag.com, August 19, 2013. Retrieved August 20, 2013 (http://www.pcmag.com/article2/0,2817,2423200,00.asp).

Hutchinson, Lee. "Review: Lego Mindstorms EV3 Means Giant Robots, Powerful Computers." Ars Technica, August 6, 2013. Retrieved August 8, 2013 (http://arstechnica.com/gadgets/2013/08/review-lego-mindstorms-ev3-means-giant-robots-powerful-computers).

Kelly, James Floyd. *LEGO Mindstorms NXT-G Programming Guide*. New York, NY: Apress, 2007.

Lidz, Franz. "How Lego Is Constructing the Next Generation of Engineers." Smithsonian.com, May 2013. Retrieved August 5, 2013 (http://www.smithsonianmag.com/ideas-innovations/How-Lego-Is-Constructing-the-Next-Generation-of-Engineers-204137981.html).

The Logo Foundation. "Programmable Brick from Lego." Logo Update Online, Fall 1998. Retrieved August 28, 2013 (http://el.media.mit.edu/logo-foundation/pubs/logoupdate/v7n1/v7n1-pbrick.html).

Meckstroth, Meghan. "Robotics 4-1-1: Four Platforms for One Prototype in One Month or Less." National Instruments, May 1, 2012. Retrieved August 25, 2013 (http://www.ni.com/white-paper/9079/en/#toc1).

MIT Media Lab. "Lego's Mindstorms." Massachusetts Institute of Technology. Retrieved July 30, 2013 (http://www.media.mit.edu/sponsorship/gettingvalue/collaborations/mindstorms).

Mortensen, Tine Froberg. "Lego History Timeline." The Lego Group, January 9, 2012. Retrieved July 20, 2013 (http://aboutus.Lego.com/en-us/Lego-group/the_Lego_history).

NPR.org. "Silicon Valley Keenly Awaits Latest Lego Robot Kit." AugOust 18, 2013. Retrieved August 26, 2013 (www.npr.org/templates/story/story.php?storyId=213178806).

Riggs, Ransom. "The Early History of Lego." Mental Floss, August 20, 2008. Retrieved August 1, 2013 (http://mentalfloss.com/article/19400/early-history-Lego).

Trangbæk, Roar Rude. "New Smarter, Stronger Lego Mindstorms EV3." The Lego Group, January 7, 2013. Retrieved July 5, 2013 (http://aboutus.lego.com/en-us/news-room/2013/january/new-smarter-stronger-lego-mindstorms-ev3).

Valk, Laurens. "EV3 and NXT: Difference and Compatibility." Robot Square, July 16, 2013. Retrieved July 30, 2013 (http://robotsquare.com/2013/07/16/ev3-nxt-compatibility).

Wolverton, Troy. "Lego Builds a Winner with New Mindstorms Robot Set." San Jose Mercury News, August 23, 2013. Retrieved August 29, 2013 (http://www.mercurynews.com/troy-wolverton/ci_23930823/wolverton-lego-builds-winner-new-mindstorms-robot-set).

{ INDEX

A

ARM 9-based processor, 17

B

bricks
creation of (interlocking), 8–9
programmable, 11, 17–19, 23–33
traditional, 9, 13

C

classroom instruction, 12, 13, 16,
    20–21, 38, 47–49, 50
command blocks
Display, 30–32
Loop, 32–33
Move, 27–28
Record/Play, 28–29
Sound, 29
Switch, 33
Wait, 30
constructivist theory of learning, 13
contests and tournaments, 38–42

D

data logging, 19, 48
data wires, 31, 35

E

educators, 12, 15, 20–21, 38, 47–49

F

First Lego League (FLL), 40–41
FIRST Robotics Competition (FRC), 42
FIRST Tech Challenge (FTC), 41–42

G

graphical programming, 11, 24,
    45–46, 48

I

Intelligent Brick, 11, 17–19, 23–24,
    26–31

J

Junior FIRST Lego League (Jr.FLL), 40

K

Kristiansen, Godfred, 9, 51
Kristiansen, Kjeld Kirk, 9
Kristiansen, Ole Kirk, 8–9

L

Lego
English translation of, 9
founding of, 8
programming language, 11
Legosheets, 11
Lego TC Logo, 10, 11
Lego Technics, 13
Lego WeDo, 13, 40
Linux operating system, 17, 49

ABOUT THE AUTHOR

Therese Shea, an author and former educator, has written over one hundred books on a wide variety of subjects. Her most recent have delved into hot topics in technology, including robotics clubs, gamification, cyberbullying, and a biography of Apple cofounder Steve Jobs. She holds degrees from Providence College and the State University of New York at Buffalo. The author currently resides in Atlanta, Georgia, with her husband, Mark.

PHOTO CREDITS

Cover The Washington Post/Getty Images; p. 5 Bloomberg/Getty Images; p. 8 Ana Nance/Redux; pp. 10–11, 19 © AP Images; p. 12 Echo/Cultura/Getty Images; p. 14 Bill Pierce/Time & Life Pictures/Getty Images; p. 16 Lego/AP Images; p. 22 Rex Features via AP Images; p. 25 Hugo12/Wikimedia Commons/File: NXT-brique.jpg/CC BY-SA 3.0; p. 28 Scientistmohamed/Wikimedia Commons/File:==MultipleViews NXT Forklift==.jpg /CC BY-SA 3.0; p. 30 LAIF/Redux; p. 32 Chen Ws/Shutterstock.com; pp. 36, 44 Tony Avelar/AP Images for LEGO Systems, Inc.; p. 37 NASA/JPL-Caltech/MSSS; p. 39 © Marco Ciavolino, courtesy of FIRST; p. 41 Jim Watson/AFP/Getty Images; p. 50 Kenneth Kua; cover and interior design elements © iStockphoto.com/letoakin (program-ming language), © iStockphoto.com/AF-studio (binary pattern), © iStockphoto.com/piccerella (crosshatch pattern).

Designer: Nicole Russo; Editor: Nicholas Croce;
Photo Researcher: Marty Levick